THIS BOOK
WAS PRESENTED TO:

_____

FROM:

_____

ON THIS DAY:

_____

_____

DESTINATION DIG

DEVOTIONS TO UNEARTH THE TRUTH ABOUT JESUS

written by
Carol Tomlinson

B&H kids

BHKids.com
Nashville, Tennessee

INTRODUCTION

Have you ever wondered if the stories and places in the Bible are real? Do you wonder how people lived during Jesus' time on earth? Me too. So it's exciting to learn about real pieces of the past that reveal the truth about who Jesus is and why He came. Over the last several decades many amazing discoveries have been made in Israel that provide solid evidence that the stories in the Bible are real!

Archaeologists have compared archaeology (the study of human history through the discovery and exploration of remains such as pottery, tools, buildings, etc.) to working a puzzle without the picture on the lid. They search for the right pieces or clues to the past to help them learn about people and how they lived. Sometimes they must very carefully dig and brush away layers of dirt just to find a small piece of pottery or an artifact. Then they continue to search for more pieces until they find enough pieces to put together and start forming a picture. Just like working a puzzle! The whole picture may not be clear at first, but if they keep searching, eventually all the pieces fit together.

Sometimes searching for the truth about Jesus feels like working a puzzle without seeing the whole picture too! But Jeremiah 29:13 tells us that if we seek and search with all our hearts, we will find Him. As you dig into these devotions, you will uncover the truth about who Jesus is, why He came, and how He lived.

PREP FOR THE DIG

Use these expert tips to help you use this devotional and dig deeper into God's Word (the Bible).

SURVEY THE SITE—Look around your home and find the perfect site to pull away and study each devotion. Maybe it's the family room, a bedroom, or a cozy spot on the porch. Anywhere you can have some quiet, uninterrupted time will work.

GRAB THE RIGHT TOOLS—Stock your site with this devotional, a Bible, pen or pencils, and a highlighter. A small notebook or journal might come in handy to record any additional thoughts or discoveries you make.

EXCAVATE—Read the Scripture verse and the devotion. Think about what the verse tells you about Jesus and how it applies to you.

CATALOG YOUR FINDS—Record your thoughts, feelings, and ideas about what you read.

SEEK AND FIND

You will seek me and find me when you search for me with all your heart.—Jeremiah 29:13

Do you like to play hide-and-seek? How about searching for lost treasure? Have you ever searched for something that you misplaced, like a favorite toy? How long would you search for a missing toy? A pet? Money? Sometimes how hard and how long we search is based on how much we value the thing we are searching for. If it is a beloved pet or maybe money, we often put in a lot of effort to find it. Sometimes searching is fun, like finding a friend in a game of hide-and-seek. But sometimes searching can be hard, especially if you can't find what you are looking for. God wants us to know and believe in His Son, Jesus. The Bible promises if we look for Him with all our hearts, we will find Him. Jesus is the most important thing we will ever search for, and the best news is that He wants to be found!

DIG DEEPER

Read these verses and fill in the blanks to discover what God has to say about seeking Him.

1 Chronicles 16:11   Seek Him _____.

Psalm 119:2   Seek Him with _____.

Matthew 6:33   Seek Him _____.

Note: You can check your answers on page 208.

PRAY

Thank God that He doesn't want to stay hidden from you; He wants you to find and know His Son, Jesus. Ask God to help you keep searching and seeking with all your heart.

THE GOOD SHEPHERD

The Lord is my shepherd;
I have what I need. —*Psalm 23:1*

We don't often think about shepherds much today, but being a shepherd was one of the main jobs in Jesus' time. A shepherd often spent a lot of time alone in fields watching over a bunch of unruly sheep. He made sure the sheep went in the right direction to find the best fields for grazing and water to drink. He kept the sheep safe from predators such as wolves. Shepherds provided all the things the sheep needed to live.

Psalm 23 is often titled "The Good Shepherd." Go ahead and check your Bible to see if that title is used. Do you know who the Good Shepherd is? That's right, the Good Shepherd is Jesus! Just like a shepherd cares for his flock and gives the sheep everything they need, Jesus cares for His flock—us! Notice I said, "everything they need" not everything they *want*. Jesus is our Shepherd. He keeps us safe, He directs our paths, and He supplies all our needs.

DIG DEEPER

Read John 10:11–16 to learn about a time when Jesus again described Himself as the Good Shepherd. In the space below, list the different ways Jesus describes a shepherd in these verses.

Write down some of the things you need below. When you feel worried that you may not have some of the things you listed, quote Psalm 23:1 to yourself as a reminder that Jesus is your Shepherd and will take care of you.

A Good Shepherd   *Things I Need*

_____   _____

_____   _____

_____   _____

_____   _____

PRAY

Read over the list you made describing a good shepherd and your list of needs. Ask God to provide for each of the things you listed, in His time and in the way that is best. Thank Jesus for caring for you and all your needs.

AT JUST THE RIGHT TIME

*For a child will be born for us, a son
will be given to us.—Isaiah 9:6*

Hannah was excited. Her birthday was coming, and she couldn't wait to celebrate with her friends. She and her mom had been planning for weeks. They mailed out invitations, ordered a cake, and bought decorations. But it seemed like the days and weeks before her party were going by so slowly. Each day seemed like a month. Hannah thought the day of her party would never arrive.

Waiting can be hard. But imagine waiting about seven hundred years for something to happen. Talk about time passing slowly! That's exactly what happened from the time Isaiah told the people of Israel that Jesus would be born until the time it happened. You can read about Jesus' birth in Matthew 1. God waited until just the right time to send Jesus to be our Savior. God's timing is perfect. He had a plan. He knew since time began that He would send Jesus, His Son, to earth to save us from our sins. God has a plan for you too. Even though waiting can be hard, you can be sure that God will fulfill His plan for you at just the right time!

DIG DEEPER

Part of God's plan for your life is to believe Jesus is His Son—that He came, lived a perfect life, and died on the cross as punishment for our sin—and to trust Jesus as your Savior. Maybe that time has already come; if so, write about how that happened below. If not, it's okay to wait for God's perfect timing. He will let you know when the time is right. Until then, write down some questions you have about trusting Jesus.

PRAY

When you feel like things aren't happening in time, remember that God's timing is perfect. Ask God to help you wait for Him to show you His plan. Thank Him for sending Jesus to be our Savior.

WHAT'S IN A NAME?

He will be named Wonderful Counselor, Mighty God, Eternal Father, Prince of Peace.—Isaiah 9:6

My friend Thomas is called Junior by his family because he and his dad have the exact same name and he is younger. My friend, Josie is named after her Grandma Josephine. And my friend Red, well her name is really Molly, but everyone calls her Red because she has red hair. We have all been given a name and sometimes even a nickname. Names sometimes tell people a little about who we are or where we come from.

Jesus is called by many names, and each one tells us something about who He is. In Isaiah 9 we see several different names that describe who Jesus is. He is the Wonderful Counselor, Mighty God, Eternal Father, and Prince of Peace, but that is not all He is. Before Jesus was born, an angel told Joseph to name the baby *Jesus*, which means He would save His people from their sins (Matthew 1:21). In Isaiah 7:14, God says His name will be *Immanuel*, which means God with us (Matthew 1:23). Immanuel is one of my favorite names for Jesus because it reminds me that He is with us; we are never alone.

DIG DEEPER

Ask your parents about how you got your name or nickname. Write each letter of your name one under the other in the space below. Next to each letter write a word that describes who you are or what you do that starts with that letter. For example, if your name is Thomas you might write the word *thoughtful* next to the T.

PRAY

Thank God that Jesus is the Savior who will save His people and for always being with us. Pray for your friends and family by name. Thank God for placing each of them in your life.

ARTIFACT CHECK

The last two devotions came from the book of Isaiah. You may remember that Isaiah wrote about Jesus seven hundred years before He was born, and that was more than two thousand years ago. With all the time that has passed, you may find it hard to believe that the book of Isaiah or even the Bible itself is real. But did you know archaeologists have found actual proof, the kind that you can see and touch, proving that the things described in Isaiah are real?

In the late 1940s, a shepherd made an amazing discovery in a cave in Qumran (an area close to the Dead Sea). The shepherd had left his flock to look for a stray goat. As he was searching, he came across a cave. He threw a rock into the cave and was surprised to hear breaking pottery. What he discovered was a collection of pottery jars. Inside the pottery jars were seven scrolls that were the first discoveries of what became known as the Dead Sea Scrolls. One of the scrolls—the Great Isaiah Scroll—dated back to about 125 BC and contained all sixty-six chapters of Isaiah. That's right, the very same book you were just reading verses from!

Over the next ten years, more caves were discovered with more scrolls and fragments. And another cave was found just a few years ago! Altogether, the Dead Sea Scrolls include more than 100,000 scrolls and fragments from 900 different texts in three different languages: Hebrew, Aramaic, and Greek. Only about a quarter of the texts were books of the Old Testament, and copies of every book were found except for Esther. These amazing discoveries are just part of the artifacts archaeologists have examined that prove the events written about in the Bible are true.

ONE WAY

Jesus told him, "I am the way, the truth, and the life. No one comes to the Father except through me."—John 14:6

Emily and her parents were planning a trip from their home in Tennessee to see the Grand Canyon. They had a map, travel guides, their computers, and their phones with GPS to help them map out which way they should go. Each item they looked at gave them a different direction to take. One mapped out the way to go based on exciting landmarks they could see as they traveled, another mapped out the shortest route, and still another told them how to get there taking only back roads and highways. It all seemed very confusing with so many ways to get to where they wanted to go; they wondered which way was the best way.

The good news for us is we don't have to wonder which way to go to get to heaven. People may try to tell you there are many different paths to get to heaven. They may tell you to just be a good person or to do more good things than bad, but the truth is there is only one way—believing that Jesus is God's Son, He lived a sinless life, and He died to take the punishment for our sins.

DIG DEEPER

Jesus is the only way to heaven, and the Bible is our map for following Him. By reading the Bible, you are learning the truth about who Jesus is and how He wants you to live. Many verses in the book of John tell you who Jesus is. Sometimes these verses are called the *I am* statements because they start with the words *I am*. Grab a highlighter and read through John. Highlight every verse you find that starts with *I am*. Challenge yourself to memorize a few of these verses to remind you who Jesus is.

PRAY

Ask God to help you read and follow His map, the Bible, every day. Thank God that He made the way to heaven clear by sending Jesus to show us the way.

JESUS IS OUR SUBSTITUTE

He made the one who did not know sin to be
sin for us, so that in him we might become the
righteousness of God.—2 Corinthians 5:21

Have you ever been working a puzzle but when you were almost finished you realized a piece was missing? What did you do? Did you look for the missing piece? Or try to find a piece to substitute for the missing piece? Did you give up and leave the puzzle incomplete? Could you put just any piece into the puzzle and call it complete? No matter what piece we try to substitute for the missing one, it won't work. We need the exact piece that fits to make our puzzle complete.

God knew we needed someone to take our sins and be a substitute for us. He knew that our sin would keep us separated from Him and that we would need a substitute to make us righteous or right with Him. In all His loving kindness, God sent Jesus to be our substitute. Jesus lived a perfect life so He could take our punishment and set us right with God. He is the only substitute we need!

DIG DEEPER

Personalizing scripture with your name is a great way to help you think about what the verse means to you personally. Putting your name in a verse can also help you pray. Substitute your name in the blanks of the verse below.

He made the one who did not
know sin to be sin for _____,
so that in him _____
might become the righteousness of God.
—2 Corinthians 5:21

PRAY

Read the verse with your name in the blanks. Thank God that He sent Jesus to be your perfect substitute and to do for you what you could not do for yourself.

WHO IS IN CHARGE?

Jesus came near and said to them, "All authority has been given to me in heaven and on earth."—Matthew 28:18

Stacey's parents were going out for dinner and a movie. They decided to put Stacey in charge of making sure her younger sister, Amanda, and their younger brother got dinner, baths, and homework finished while their parents were out. Amanda didn't think it was fair to leave Stacey in charge. Stacey was only two years older, and she always got to be the one in charge. Amanda wanted a chance to be the one in charge for once. She wanted to have the power and authority to tell her brother and sister what to do and have them do as she said.

Jesus is in charge of everything. He has been given all authority over heaven and earth by His Father. In Mark 4:35–41, Jesus told the wind and sea to be still during a storm. And guess what? They obeyed! If the wind and seas are under Jesus' authority, we should be too. The good thing is we can trust Jesus' authority for our good. He will never tell us to do anything that would go against what pleases God.

DIG DEEPER

Think about who has authority in your life. Your parents. Your teacher. The principal at your school. Many people may hold a position of authority or be in charge, but Jesus is the overall One in charge. One way you can please God is to obey those who have authority over you. Use the space below to list how you can obey each of the people listed.

My Parents	*My Teachers*	*Jesus*

PRAY

Thank God that He gave Jesus authority over everything. Ask God to help you please Him by obeying those He has placed in charge of you.

THE CREATOR

For everything was created by him, in heaven and on earth, the visible and the invisible, whether thrones or dominions or rulers or authorities—all things have been created through him and for him.—Colossians 1:16

Peyton and Casin were on a family vacation at the beach. Each night they went outside, listened to the waves as they crashed on the shore, and gazed up at the stars in the sky. One night they even took flashlights and a pail to look for crabs in the sand. Their mom pointed out just how amazing God's creation is—the bright moon and stars, the vast ocean, and the funny little crabs that scurry sideways on the sand.

God is the Creator of everything. Starting with nothing, He created all the things we can see and those we can't see. He didn't need to have supplies on hand to start His creation. He just spoke and it came to be. He created everything—including you and me—to be just as He wanted it to be.

DIG DEEPER

Read Genesis 1. This chapter tells us all about creation. Circle these words in the puzzle to remind you of some amazing things in creation: *seas, people, bugs, stars, fish, plants, sun, light, birds, flowers, animals,* and *moon.*

```
S  P  N  X  G  L  O  H  M  O  O  N  L  I  G  P  H
S  E  A  S  W  S  S  P  L  A  N  T  S  I  O  P  L
M  O  B  D  E  T  J  F  L  O  W  E  R  S  G  O  Y
S  P  Z  U  F  A  N  I  M  A  L  S  K  U  B  H  F
R  L  I  J  G  R  D  S  S  W  A  X  Y  N  B  I  T
P  E  K  L  M  S  G  H  R  P  I  B  I  R  D  S  U
```

Note: You can check your answers on page 208.

PRAY

Look around and make a list of everything you can see that God created. Read down your list, stop after each item, and praise Him for creating so many wonderful things.

OUR ADVOCATE

My little children, I am writing you these things so that you may not sin. But if anyone does sin, we have an advocate with the Father—Jesus Christ the righteous one.—1 John 2:1

Do you have a good friend who sticks up for you no matter what? Someone who has your back and is always by your side? A friend who always picks you to be on his team and tells others how great you are even when you mess up? You might call that friend an *advocate*. An advocate is someone who speaks up for you. They try to make things better for you.

Whether you know it or not, you do have a friend like that—Jesus! In 1 John 2:1 the Bible says Jesus is your advocate with God. That means when you mess up, Jesus is right there telling God how great you are and pleading your case. Jesus doesn't tell you it's okay to sin, but He's telling you that when you sin He will be your advocate and make things right with God because He already paid the price for your sins.

DIG DEEPER

Proverbs 18:24 says "There is a friend who stays closer than a brother." No matter how many friends you have, one definitely fits that description—Jesus! Not only is Jesus our advocate, but He is also a friend who will never leave us. No matter what we go through, Jesus is right there by our side. Make a list of the people who are your advocates: parents, brothers and sisters, friends, and, most importantly, Jesus.

_____

_____

_____

_____

_____

PRAY

Thank God for the people in your life who are your advocates and for Jesus, who stays by your side no matter what.

10

WHOSE SON ARE YOU?

They all asked, "Are you, then, the Son of God?" And
he said to them, "You say that I am."—Luke 22:70

Has anyone ever asked if you are someone's son or daughter?
Maybe they asked, "Are you Bobby's son?" or are you "Betty's
daughter?" One of the ways people identify you is by family—
as someone's son, daughter, brother, sister, and so on. Part of
our identities is based on the family we belong to. When we
go out into the world, we represent our parents and our entire
families too.

Jesus was asked, "Whose Son are You?" many times. People
wanted to know if He really was the Son of God they had been
waiting for. In Matthew 3:17, God Himself identifies Jesus as His
Son. God told the crowd who witnessed Jesus' baptism, "This is
my beloved Son, with whom I am well-pleased." Not only did God
confirm Jesus' identity as His Son, He let the people know He
was pleased with how Jesus represented His Father in the world.

DIG DEEPER

Did you know that if you are a follower of Jesus then you are God's son or daughter too? Well, you are! Read 1 John 3:1. Who does the verse say we are? That's right—we are the children of God! Think about who you are and how people can identify you as a child of God. Write your name below. Then draw an equal sign and write "Child of God" after the sign.

PRAY

Thank God that you are His child and part of His family. If you have not yet become a follower of Jesus, pray that God will show you when the time is right, and that He will help you find answers to any questions you have.

KING OF KINGS

And he has a name written on his robe and on his thigh:
KING OF KINGS AND LORD OF LORDS.—Revelation 19:16

When I was a kid, we played a game called King of the Mountain. The object of the game was to be the person standing on top of a small hill (or a mound of pillows if we were inside). One person would be the king and stand on top of the mountain, and everyone else tried to push him off the top to become the king. As you can imagine, kings changed often.

There are many kings whose rules have been recorded in the Bible. Some of those kings reigned for many years, like King Manasseh, who ruled over Judah for fifty-five years. Others like King Zimri, whose rule was only seven days, ruled for a short time. But Jesus is the King of kings, which means He is above all other kings. In Daniel 7:13–14, Jesus' rule and His kingdom are described as lasting forever. He's one King who won't change.

DIG DEEPER

If you had a king or queen ruling over you, what would you want him to be like? Would you want someone who was kind, who cared about the people he ruled over, or maybe someone who was fair? You can be sure that Jesus is all those things and more. He is the perfect King! In the space below, draw a picture of what you think a good king looks like.

PRAY

Thank God for making Jesus the perfect King to rule forever.

CATALOG YOUR FINDS

When archaeologists make a discovery, or a *find* as they call it, they will take the find and catalog it. This means they will record the section of the dig site where the item was found, along with photographs or drawings and any other important information that helps them identify the item.

In the previous devotions you have discovered a lot of information about who the Bible says Jesus is. Use these pages to catalog your finds. Answer the questions, and fill in the spaces provided. Add any notes or drawings that will help you identify who Jesus is.

What description of Jesus did you like the most? Why?

What verse was your favorite?

Try to memorize it and highlight it in your Bible.

If someone asked you, who would you say Jesus is?

ARTIFACT CHECK

Remember when you read about Jesus being your advocate? And how an advocate is someone who stands up for you and fights to make things better for you? Well, Israel had a king named David who was an advocate for them long before he became king. You might remember the story about the time David took on a giant named Goliath. Did you know that archaeologists have found proof that giants like Goliath (he is believed to have been 9 feet 9 inches tall) really did exist and live in a city called Gath?

It's true! The site of the city was first discovered in 1899, but it wasn't until 2015 that the discovery of giant gates, a building for making weapons, a temple, and inscriptions that mention two names that are similar to Goliath were found. This discovery was further proof that the story of David and Goliath in 1 Samuel 17 is not a myth or a fairy tale—it is true!

The size of the gates discovered suggest that the people who lived in the city of Gath were taller and bigger than those in the surrounding cities. The blocks used to build the gates are about 13 feet tall and 6½ to 8 feet wide, big enough for a giant like Goliath to pass through. These were much taller and wider than blocks used to build walls and gates around other cities during the time. The city itself is believed to cover 123.5 acres. One football field is 1.32 acres. That means you would have to put almost 94 football fields together to be the size of Gath. That's what I call a big discovery!

THE IMPOSSIBLE

For I passed on to you as most important what I also received: that Christ died for our sins according to the Scriptures, that he was buried, that he was raised on the third day according to the Scriptures.—1 Corinthians 15:3–4

Have you ever heard the phrase, "Looking for a needle in a hay-stack"? It basically means that you are looking for something that is going to be very hard to find. Imagine looking for something as small as a needle in a big stack of hay! That would seem nearly impossible.

A few pages back you read some verses from the book of Isaiah and learned about the Great Isaiah Scroll. Many of the verses in Isaiah are prophecies (a message inspired by God) that told about Jesus' birth, life, and death. When Jesus was born, He fulfilled more than three hundred of the prophecies written in the Old Testament. The chances of all those prophecies being fulfilled in one person is nearly impossible. In fact, the chance of fulfilling eight of the prophecies is one in a quintillion (100,000,000,000,000,000).

DIG DEEPER

Jesus came so the prophecies written in the Old Testament would be fulfilled or come to be. Read the New Testament verses below to discover how Jesus fulfilled the prophecies. Place a check mark next to each New Testament verse once you read it. Circle the one you find most amazing.

Old Testament Prophecy	New Testament Fulfillment
Jesus will be born in Bethlehem.—Micah 5:2	Luke 2:4–7
The blind will see, the deaf will hear, the lame will leap, and the mute will speak.—Isaiah 35:5–6	Matthew 9:35
The Messiah will ride a donkey into Jerusalem while the people shout.—Zechariah 9:9	John 12:12–15
A friend will betray Jesus for thirty pieces of silver.—Zechariah 11:12–13	Matthew 26:14–15

PRAY

Praise God for doing the impossible. Thank God for sending Jesus to fulfill all His prophecies so we can trust Jesus as our Savior.

GROWING UP

And Jesus increased in wisdom and stature, and in favor with God and with people.—Luke 2:52

Every year on Maddie's birthday, her grandmother marked Maddie's height on the doorframe in her kitchen. Maddie liked to see the marks and how much she had grown each year. She grew two inches between her tenth and eleventh birthdays. Maddie's grandmother reminded her that growing taller and stronger is important, but not as important as growing in how much she knew about the Bible and Jesus.

Jesus grew taller and stronger each year too. That is what Luke 2:52 is referring to when it says, "Jesus increased in . . . stature." But notice that the verse also says Jesus increased in wisdom and in favor with God and with people. Jesus went to the temple and listened to the teachers. He read and memorized the Old Testament Scriptures. He continued to do the things that please God. All these things helped Him grow in more than just height and strength.

DIG DEEPER

Marking your height on a chart is fun and is a good reminder of how much you have grown. Instead of a height chart, ask an adult to help you make a chart to keep track of Bible verses you read or memorize. You might be surprised to look back on your chart and see how you have grown in wisdom and favor with God. Use the verses below to help you get started.

John 3:16   Deuteronomy 6:5   Proverbs 3:5

Jeremiah 29:13   Matthew 20:28   Romans 1:16

PRAY

Ask God to help you grow in your knowledge of the Bible and Jesus. Pray that He will give you the ability to read and understand the Bible.

GOOD NEWS

But he said to them, "It is necessary for me to proclaim the good news about the kingdom of God to the other towns also, because I was sent for this purpose."—Luke 4:43

Parker was so excited. He got the lead role in the play at school, and he couldn't wait to share the good news with his parents and grandparents. When his mom picked him up from school, Parker excitedly told her all about trying out for the play and getting the lead role. When he and his mom arrived home, they immediately called his grandparents to tell them the good news.

One of the reasons Jesus came was to proclaim or tell people the good news about the kingdom of God. He wanted people to have hope and to know what wonderful things waited for them in God's kingdom. But Jesus didn't have a cell phone, social media, or even newspapers. To tell people the good news, He had to walk from town to town. Jesus shared the message with people, and those people shared the message with more people. That's how the good news traveled during Jesus' time.

DIG DEEPER

How do you share good news? How do you think you can share the good news about Jesus and God's kingdom with your friends? Will you write them a letter, talk to them on the playground, call them on the phone, or invite them to church? In the space below plan how you can tell someone what you know about Jesus.

Who I will tell:

_____

My plan:

_____

_____

_____

_____

PRAY

Ask God to give you the courage to speak out and share what you know about Jesus.

BEING HUMBLE

He humbled himself by becoming obedient to the point
of death—even to death on a cross.—Philippians 2:8

Joe always bragged about everything. He loved to tell people how he was the star of his soccer team. On the field he never passed the ball to any of the other players even if they could score a goal for the team. Joe always wanted to be the first in line when the snacks were handed out after the game. He never let anyone go before him or helped pick up the gear after practice.

Jesus had every right to be proud; after all, He is God's Son. Jesus could have boasted that He is in control of everything. He could have bragged about being the King of kings, but Jesus did not do any of that. He was humble, which means He put others before Himself. Jesus lived a perfectly sinless life and considered Himself a servant, even to the point of dying in our place.

DIG DEEPER

In Mark 10:45, Jesus tells His disciples that even though He was God's Son, He came to serve others, not to be served. Think about how you can be humble and put the needs of someone else before your own. Listed below are a few possible answers. Circle one or two that you could do.

- Let someone go before you in line.
- Open the door for someone.
- Pass the ball to someone on your team.
- Share your candy with a friend.
- Let your brother or sister go first in a game.
- Take someone's tray or dish to the sink.
- Offer to help your teacher clean the classroom.
- Help someone in your family with a chore.

PRAY

Thank Jesus for living humbly and setting an example for how you should live. Ask Him to help you think of ways to be humble and serve others.

16
A GOOD TEACHER

"You call me Teacher and Lord—and you are speaking rightly, since that is what I am. So if I, your Lord and Teacher, have washed your feet, you also ought to wash one another's feet. For I have given you an example, that you also should do just as I have done for you."—John 13:13–15

Jamie's favorite teacher was Mrs. Pickard. She didn't just tell you how to do things, she showed you. When Jamie didn't understand how to work a math problem, Mrs. Pickard would sit with her and work examples to show Jamie how to get the answer to the problem. Mrs. Pickard was patient and kind to everyone. She showed Jamie how to treat others with kindness too. Jamie learned a lot from Mrs. Pickard because she was a good teacher.

A good teacher sets an example you can follow. Jesus was referred to as Teacher in many different places in the Bible. In Jesus' time on earth, people's feet often got dirty and dusty because they wore sandals and walked everywhere. The host of the home would often have someone wash and dry his guests' feet before they entered the house. Jesus washed His disciples' feet as an example to teach His disciples how to serve one another. Jesus is more than just a good teacher; He is the greatest Teacher ever!

DIG DEEPER

Think about someone who is a good teacher and sets a good example for you. It could be a teacher at school or church, a parent, grandparent, or neighbor. Use the space below to write what makes that person a good teacher. Write a thank-you note to thank him or her for being a good example and a good teacher.

PRAY

Thank God for placing good teachers in your life. Praise Jesus for being the greatest Teacher and example to follow.

17
WHO NEEDS A DOCTOR?

Jesus replied to them, "It is not those who are healthy who need a doctor, but those who are sick."—Luke 5:31

Have you ever been sick and needed a doctor? I don't mean like a few sniffles that your mom gives you medicine for at home. I am talking about being so sick you needed a doctor to help you feel better. Sometimes when we are sick, we can take care of ourselves. Other times we need someone else to give us what we need to get better.

However, there is one sickness we can't heal, no matter what we do or how many doctors we see. It's called sin. Sin entered the world way back in the garden of Eden when Adam chose to disobey God. You can read about it in Genesis 3. God knew we couldn't save ourselves from our sins; that's why He sent Jesus to save us. Jesus is the only One we need to cure us from sin.

DIG DEEPER

Think about the people you know who are sick. Although you cannot heal them, you can tell them about Jesus and pray for them to get better. Now think about someone who needs to know that Jesus can save us from our sin. Write that person's initials below and plan to pray for him or her every day.

PRAY

Ask God to heal those who are sick physically, and pray for people who do not know about Jesus. Pray that God will give you a chance to tell them about the One who can save them from their sin.

18

SHOW GOD'S POWER

If this man were not from God, he wouldn't
be able to do anything.—John 9:33

When you hear the word *mud*, what do you think about? Maybe you think about mud puddles, making mud pies, or how mud is used to make bricks. But do you think about using mud to heal someone? Sounds strange to me. But that's exactly what Jesus did in John 9. He spat in the dirt and made mud. Then Jesus rubbed the mud on the eyes of a man who had been born blind. After placing the mud on the man's eyes, Jesus told the man to go wash his eyes in the Pool of Siloam. Immediately after the man washed his eyes, he could see!

Jesus came to show God's power and bring glory to God through the miracles He performed. Because these events were recorded in the Bible, we can trust that Jesus is God's Son, and He has the power to do what seems impossible.

DIG DEEPER

Jesus performed many miracles in His ministry. Look up the verses below about other miracles Jesus performed. Fill in the blanks.

1. Jesus made a paralyzed man _____.
   (Matthew 9:1–8)
2. Jesus restored a man's shriveled _____.
   (Matthew 12:10–13)
3. Jesus fed five thousand men with ____ loaves of bread and ____ fish. (Matthew 14:15–21)
4. Jesus raised Lazarus from the _____.
   (John 11:1–46)
5. Jesus restored the _____ of the high priest's servant. (Luke 22:50–51)

Note: You can check your answers on page 208.

PRAY

Every miracle Jesus performed brought glory to God and demonstrated His power over all things. Praise God for sending Jesus to show us how powerful He is. Thank Him for having power over everything.

ARTIFACT CHECK

You may remember that Jesus told the blind man to go wash the mud from his eyes in the Pool of Siloam and the man's vision was restored. What you may not know is that the Pool of Siloam is a real place. This wasn't like a swimming pool where you might go to swim and float around on a sunny day. Near the City of David in Jerusalem, the Pool of Siloam was a pool of water filled by a spring. The pool was commonly used as a cleansing pool or a place where people washed away anything unclean from their bodies.

In 2004, construction workers uncovered the steps leading into the Pool of Siloam as they were repairing a drainage pipe. The repairs were stopped, and archaeologists dug through ten feet of mud to discover another set of steps and a 225-foot-long pool. That's about the wingspan from the tip of one wing to the tip of the other wing on a 747 jet airplane. The pool has three sets of five steps that lead down to a platform before reaching the bottom, and it is shaped like a trapezoid.

To determine when the pool was made, archaeologists used metal detectors to find coins and other artifacts nearby. These artifacts helped the archaeologists determine that the pool was

most likely built hundreds of years before Jesus was born. The pool was still in use until the Romans conquered Jerusalem. The discovery of the pool suggests that the events written about in the book of John really happened and were not just made up as some people believe.

19

PREPARING A PLACE

In my Father's house are many rooms. If it were
not so, would I have told you that I am going
to prepare a place for you?—John 14:2

Kallie's family is moving to a new house. Her parents met with
builders to plan out how many rooms would be in the house and
what each room would be used for. Kallie was excited because
she was going to get her own bedroom, and her mom said she
could plan how she wanted it to look. Kallie spent a lot of time
preparing for her room. She picked out just the right color for the
walls, the right place for her bookshelf, and the perfect quilt to go
on her bed. Kallie couldn't wait to tell her friends about her new
house and room.

Jesus came to tell us about His Father's house and to let us
know He is preparing for us to join Him there someday. There will
be room for everyone who trusts Jesus and accepts His gift of
salvation. We can believe this is true because Jesus told us it is!

DIG DEEPER

If you were preparing a place for someone, what would you include? Draw a picture of what you think would be the perfect place.

PRAY

Thank Jesus for coming to tell us about the place He is preparing for us to live with God forever.

COMFORT

> Blessed be the God and Father of our Lord Jesus Christ, the Father of mercies and the God of all comfort. He comforts us in all our affliction, so that we may be able to comfort those who are in any kind of affliction, through the comfort we ourselves receive from God.—2 Corinthians 1:3–4

Have you ever heard someone say they just needed some comfort food? Sometimes when people are sad or feeling down, they want something that will bring them comfort like a favorite food that reminds them of happier times. Or maybe they want a favorite blanket to cuddle up with when they have a cold or are tired. What about you? Do you have anything that comforts you, like a favorite stuffed animal or your pet?

God sent Jesus to experience everything we do, so He can provide comfort to us when we are experiencing sadness or hard times. Although you cannot see Jesus or feel His arms around you, He can comfort you by giving you a sense of calm or peace. One way He comforts you is through people who have experienced the same things you have. And sometimes Jesus sends you to comfort others.

DIG DEEPER

Another way to feel the comfort Jesus provides is by memorizing Bible verses to repeat to yourself when you feel sad or are going through a hard time. Look up Psalm 119:76. Write the verse below and then write it on a sticky note. Stick it to your mirror where you will see it every day.

PRAY

When you need comfort, pray Psalm 119:76 and ask Jesus to give you comfort and peace.

21

REST

"Come to me, all of you who are weary and burdened,
and I will give you rest."—Matthew 11:28

Jesse was tired. He had a lot to do every day. Jesse's day started with school, where he had to focus on learning what his teacher taught and keeping up with his assignments. Then he went to soccer practice, where he had to learn all the drills and plays for his game on Saturday. From soccer practice he went home to have dinner, do his homework, and take a shower before he could finally rest. In between all his activities, Jesse worried about his family because his parents had been fighting with each other.

In Matthew when Jesus said He came to give us rest, He didn't mean just sleep or actual physical rest. Jesus came to take on the things that make us weary or burdened like worry, fear, and doubt. He will help you find peace and rest from the things that cause you to be worn out and tired. And He will even give you rest at night when you lay your head on your pillow.

DIG DEEPER

Psalm 55:22 and 1 Peter 5:7 tell us to cast all our cares upon the Lord because He cares about us. That means you can tell Jesus about anything that is bothering you or making you weary. In the space below list some of the things that worry you.

PRAY

Read through the list you wrote. Pray and ask Jesus to take your burdens and give you rest from worrying about them.

22
THE EAST TO THE WEST?

But you know that he appeared so that he might take away our sins. And in him is no sin.—1 John 3:5 NIV

John's Sunday school teacher read Psalm 103:12 to his class. The verse says that Jesus removed our sins as far as the east is from the west. John was confused about what this meant. He couldn't imagine how far that would be. His teacher took out a globe and pointed out that there is an actual north and south pole. So as you travel, you will eventually end in one direction and begin in another only to wind up right where you started. But if you go east to west there is no starting or ending point. Since there are no east or west poles you just continue in one direction. So in Psalm 103:12, God is giving you the idea of something being infinite, meaning it never ends.

We have read several reasons why Jesus came to live as a human. He came to heal the sick, provide comfort, teach, and to set an example for us. But those aren't the main reason. The main reason is revealed in 1 John 3:5 when it says He came to take away our sins. Jesus is the only One who can take our sins away because He never sinned. He is the only One who can take them as far as the east is from the west.

DIG DEEPER

Read through the list of sins below. Think about the ones you have committed. Then draw a big X over all of them because Jesus came to take away our sin.

Lying

Cheating

Stealing

Disobeying my parents

Talking about people behind their backs

Bullying another person

PRAY

Jesus came to take away all our sins—those we have already committed, those we will commit today, and those we will commit in the future—they are all covered! Thank Jesus for coming and taking all our sins so we can be forgiven.

WITHOUT SIN

He did not commit sin, and no deceit was
found in his mouth.—1 Peter 2:22

Meredith wanted to watch a new show coming on TV, but she had homework to finish. She only had five more problems to do. She decided it would be okay to watch the show even though she knew her mom's rule was no TV until homework was done. When her mom came through the living room and asked Meredith if she had finished all her homework, Meredith said she had. Meredith knew her answer wasn't completely true, but she figured it wasn't too bad since she only had a few problems to finish.

Telling half the truth is still a lie, and it is still a sin. Romans 3:23 says, "All have sinned and fall short of the glory of God." Jesus is the only person who never sinned. He never lied, took something that didn't belong to Him, cheated, or committed any other sin. We will never live without sins as Jesus did, but we should make it our goal to be more like Him. Ephesians 5:1 says we should be imitators of God, which means we should try to think and act as Jesus did.

DIG DEEPER

Several years ago, it was popular for people to say "WWJD." That stood for "What Would Jesus Do?" People would often ask this question to help remind them to do the right thing and follow Jesus. Use the space below to list things you can do to be more like Jesus. A few things are listed to get you started.

Pray
Help others
Be honest

_____

_____

_____

_____

PRAY

Ask God to help you be more like Jesus. Ask Him to forgive you of your sins and help you do better next time.

PLEASING JESUS

"The one who sent me is with me. He has not left me alone, because I always do what pleases him."—John 8:29

Amy's mother asked her to help weed the garden. Amy really didn't want to go outside in the heat and spend hours bent over pulling up weeds. She really wanted to go play video games with her friends, but she wanted to please her mother too. Amy thought about what choice she should make. As she was thinking, she remembered that at church her pastor talked about the way Jesus always did what pleased His Father. She wanted to be more like Jesus, so she chose to help her mom in the garden.

Jesus always did what pleased God even when He knew it was going to be hard or painful. In Mark 14, Jesus went to the garden of Gethsemane to pray. He knew He was about to be put on trial and die on a cross even though He had done nothing wrong. In His prayer, Jesus asked God if there was another way to save people from their sin. Even though Jesus knew it would be a very painful and hard thing to do, He told God He would do what God wanted Him to. Jesus knew that when He followed God's plan, He would not be alone. And when we choose to be like Jesus, we are never alone!

DIG DEEPER

Make a list of things that are hard for you to do but that please Jesus. Circle a few of the things you wrote down and do them even though they are hard.

_____

_____

_____

_____

_____

_____

_____

_____

PRAY

The next time you must choose to do something that is hard for you, pray and ask Jesus to be with you and give you strength.

ARTIFACT CHECK

Do you ever wonder if the people mentioned in the Bible really lived and did the things the Bible talks about? Many of the names and dates given for the people you read about can be found in historical documents, supporting their existence. But if you are the kind of person who needs to do more than read about something to have final proof, you are in luck.

When Jesus was arrested and sent to trial, He was taken to testify or tell His story to a man named Caiaphas. Caiaphas was a high priest in the Jewish court. Archeologists have uncovered a path of stone steps that lead from Mount Zion to the Kidron Valley. It is believed that Jesus would have most likely used this path to Gethsemane and, later, back up to Caiaphas' house where He stood trial. In 1990, workers who were widening an old road uncovered a burial site. Inside the site, archaeologists found a tomb that belonged to Caiaphas' family. This find proves that Caiaphas, the same one Jesus testified before, was a real person.

Another name that you may have heard about from Jesus' trial is Pontius Pilate. He was the governor who wanted to release Jesus but didn't because it would upset the crowd. Many people thought the writers of the Bible just made him up because they could not find out much about him in historical records. In 1961,

proof was found that Pilate was a real person. A block seat was discovered in an amphitheater, or outdoor theater, with his name inscribed in the block. The seat dated back between AD 26 and 37, which is exactly the time the Bible says Pilate was the governor of Judea.

VICTORY

The sting of death is sin, and the power of sin is the law. But thanks be to God, who gives us the victory through our Lord Jesus Christ!—1 Corinthians 15:56–57

Billy's football team was playing in the state championship. They had beaten ten other teams to make it to this game. The team had put in the hard work to practice and run plays in preparation for the game. Billy's coach talked to the players before the game and told them how this would be their biggest win yet. The whole team felt ready to go out and win the championship.

Being victorious over another team is a great thing, but it isn't a victory that will last forever. Next year there may be a new state champion. Jesus came to give us a victory that will last for eternity. He came to give us victory over sin and death. Because Jesus died on the cross and rose three days later, those who believe in Him will have eternal life in heaven when they die. That's a victory worth celebrating!

DIG DEEPER

Sometimes when a team wins the big game, they receive a trophy. The trophy usually has something engraved or written on it to help the team remember the win. Write something in the middle of the trophy below to celebrate Jesus' victory over death.

PRAY

Say a prayer of thanks to Jesus for winning the victory over sin and death.

SHOW COMPASSION

When he went ashore, he saw a large crowd, had compassion on them, and healed their sick.—Matthews 14:14

Mandy noticed that her elderly neighbor, Ms. Owens, was struggling to get her trash can to the curb in the rain. She felt bad for Ms. Owens because she lived alone and had no one to help her. Mandy was concerned that Ms. Owens might slip on her wet driveway. So Mandy went to the hall closet, got out her raincoat, and went out to help. Ms. Owens was so grateful for Mandy's help.

Jesus often acted with compassion or concern for others. The Bible tells us more than once that Jesus was "moved by compassion." This means that, like Mandy, when Jesus saw someone who was in need, He acted. He didn't walk away or leave it to someone else to take care of.

DIG DEEPER

Read the verses below about other times Jesus showed compassion and care to those He met. Check off each set of verses after you read them.

- ☐ Matthew 20:30–34
- ☐ Mark 10:13–16
- ☐ Luke 7:11–15

PRAY

Thank Jesus for being compassionate and caring. Ask Him to help you find times to show compassion and care for those around you.

CATALOG YOUR FINDS

In the previous devotions, you discovered why Jesus came and how He lived. Use these pages to catalog your finds. Answer the questions and fill in the spaces provided. Add any notes or drawings that will remind you of what you learned about why Jesus came and how He lived.

If someone asked you why Jesus came, how would you answer?

Pick one of the verses that described how Jesus lived. Write it in the space below, and read it out loud to help you memorize it.

How does it make you feel to know that Jesus came to take the punishment for your sin and to make things right with God?

ARTIFACT CHECK

Jesus spent a lot of time in a boat during His ministry. He called several of His disciples to leave their boats and jobs as fishermen to follow Him. Jesus taught from a boat, He calmed the wind and the seas from a boat, and He even slept in one during a storm. Boats are mentioned more than fifty times in Matthew, Mark, Luke, and John.

In 1986, two fishermen discovered a fishing boat that dated back to Jesus' time. The boat was found at the Sea of Galilee, a sea mentioned many times in the Bible. A severe drought or lack of rain caused the water levels of the sea to drop so low that the two fishermen were able to see the outline of the boat in the mud. Most boats that sink rot or get eaten by a clam called a shipworm. This boat stayed together because the muddy sea bottom protected it.

The boat is 27 feet long and about 7.5 feet wide. The boat was made of Lebanese cedar and oak. Even though this is not an exact boat Jesus and His disciples used, it is dated to be from the time Jesus and the disciples lived. Archaeologists looking near the boat also found a cooking pot, lamp, and other items used by people during Jesus' time.

The type of boat used in Jesus' time

27
MISSING THE MARK

For all have sinned and fall short of the glory of God; they are justified freely by his grace through the redemption that is in Christ Jesus.—Romans 3:23–24

Darren and his brother, Timmy, were at archery practice. They had their bows and arrows and were practicing hitting the bull's-eye on the target across the field. Darren's first shots went wide and missed the target entirely. Timmy's first shots hit the outside of the target, but not the bull's-eye. The more they practiced, the closer they got to the bull's-eye. By the end of practice, they still hadn't hit the bull's-eye, but their coach told them to keep practicing.

When we miss the mark or break one of God's commands, that's called sin. We all sin and fall short of the mark no matter how hard we try. Jesus is the only One who has never missed the mark or sinned. Because God is holy and heaven is perfect, anyone who sins cannot live in heaven with Him. God provided a way for us to be able to have eternal life with Him when Jesus died on the cross to pay the penalty for our sins.

DIG DEEPER

Even though we still sin and fall short of God's glory, our goal is to act more like Jesus every day. Just because we miss the mark doesn't mean we should quit trying. Write Jesus' name in the center or bull's-eye of the target below. Around the target write things you can do to act more like Jesus.

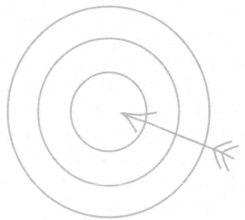

PRAY

Thank God for providing a way for you to live with Him in heaven. Ask God to help you be more like Jesus every day.

I AM SORRY

Therefore repent and turn back, so that your
sins may be wiped out.—Acts 3:19

Have your parents ever made you apologize to your brother or sister or someone else for arguing? Did you say you were sorry and mean it? Or did you say the words but not really mean them? Sometimes when we say, "I am sorry," we only say the words because it's what we have been told or taught to do. We don't really feel sorry for what we've done or change our actions to show we really are sorry.

When we tell God we are sorry and really mean it, that is called repentance. God does not want us to just say we are sorry; He wants us to change what we are doing wrong and turn to doing what is right. When we truly repent, God completely forgives us and helps us do what is right.

DIG DEEPER

Think about a sin you need to repent and turn away from. Maybe it's lying, using bad words, or fighting with others. Write down whatever it is in the center of the arrow as a reminder to turn from the wrong you are doing and repent.

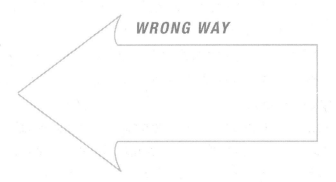

WRONG WAY

PRAY

Ask God to forgive you of the things you are doing that displease Him. Ask Him to help you change what you are doing and go the right way instead.

THE PERFECT GIFT

There is salvation in no one else, for there is
no other name under heaven given to people
by which we must be saved.—Acts 4:12

Jenna's mom planned on getting Jenna the perfect gift for her birthday. Jenna asked for a new bike to ride around the neighborhood with her friends, so her mom picked out the perfect one. It was blue with sparkly stripes and a shiny silver seat. The bike had a basket on the handlebars so Jenna could carry her water bottle and snacks. Her mom knew this bike would be perfect for her.

Sometimes we think we know what the perfect gift is. The Bible tells us that there is one perfect gift we all need, and that is salvation. And we can only receive that gift through trusting in one name—Jesus! Jesus gave up His life so we can be a part of God's family for eternity. His sacrifice is the best gift ever!

DIG DEEPER

Below are two descriptions of what makes a gift perfect. Can you add other ideas?

It's something the person really wants.

It's something the person doesn't already have.

_____

_____

_____

Now look for the book of James in your Bible. Read James 1:17. What kind of gifts does God give?

_____

Note: Check your answer on page 208.

PRAY

Thank God that all His gifts are good and perfect. Thank Jesus for giving up His life to provide us with the best gift ever.

GETTING WHAT I DESERVE

For you are saved by grace through faith, and this is not from yourselves; it is God's gift—not from works, so that no one can boast.—Ephesians 2:8–9

Jasmine's dad gave her mom a pair of new earrings. Jasmine thought they were the prettiest earrings she had ever seen and wanted to see how they would look on her. But Jasmine's mom said she could not try on the earrings because they were a special gift. When her parents went out to the store, Jasmine sneaked into their room to try on the earrings. As she was taking them out of the box, the post broke off the back of one of the earrings. Jasmine knew she was in big trouble. When her mom got home, Jasmine admitted what happened and waited for her mom's punishment. To Jasmine's surprise, her mom hugged her and told Jasmine that she would get the earring fixed.

Jasmine did not get the punishment she deserved; instead her mom extended grace and gave Jasmine what she did not deserve. That's what it means to be saved by grace. God did not give us the punishment we deserve. Instead He sent Jesus to take our punishment. And the best part of God's grace is that it is a gift, free to all who believe!

DIG DEEPER

Read Romans 3:24. Think about a time you received grace from someone. Maybe it was your parents, a teacher, or your brother or sister. Write about that time here.

_____

_____

_____

_____

_____

_____

_____

PRAY

Thank God that He does not give us what we deserve for our sins. Ask Him to help you extend grace to people around you.

BELIEVE

Jesus replied, "This is the work of God—that you believe in the one he has sent."—John 6:29

Joel and his family went to church every week. His dad was a leader in the church, and his mom taught Sunday school. Joel listened to the preacher, he did what his parents and teachers told him to do, and he even helped those who needed it. Joel figured that because he was a pretty good kid and tried to do more good than bad, he would surely get to go to heaven someday. But that's not what the Bible says.

The Bible tells us that we cannot save ourselves. We cannot pray enough, go to church enough, read our Bibles enough, or do enough good things to save ourselves from our sin problem. Believing that Jesus died for our sins and rose from the dead is the only thing that will solve our sin problem and allow us to live forever with God in heaven.

DIG DEEPER

Read these verses about what it means to believe in Jesus. Check off each verse as you read it.

- ☐ John 3:16
- ☐ John 14:6
- ☐ Acts 16:31

PRAY

If you already believe in Jesus and have placed your trust in Him, ask God to help you learn more about Him. If you are ready to place your trust in Jesus, tell God you believe and want to accept His gift of forgiveness.

I HAVE TO SEE IT TO BELIEVE IT

Jesus said, "Because you have seen me, you have believed. Blessed are those who have not seen and yet believe."—John 20:29

Sarah's friend Jeremy told her that he could jump from one side of the creek to the other in one leap. It sounded impossible. Sarah wasn't sure if she could take her friend's word for it. She told Jeremy she would believe it when she saw it with her own eyes. The next day, Sarah and Jeremy met at the creek. Jeremy went to one side and got a good running start. Then he jumped over the creek to the other side in one giant leap. Sarah was amazed and finally believed Jeremy because she saw it with her own eyes.

In the Bible, one of Jesus' disciples, Thomas, said he had to see and touch Jesus' scars before he would believe Jesus was raised from the dead. Jesus appeared to Thomas and let him touch His scars and see for himself that Jesus was alive. It's hard to believe in something or someone you can't see. When you do, that is called faith. Jesus wants you to have faith and believe in Him even when you can't see Him.

DIG DEEPER

Read the full story about doubting Thomas in John 20:24–29. Draw an eye in the space below. Then write *I don't have to see to believe in Jesus* below your drawing.

PRAY

Ask God to help you believe in Jesus even though you can't see Him.

PROMISES KEPT

None of the good promises the LORD had made to the house of Israel failed. Everything was fulfilled.—Joshua 21:45

Chelsea told her best friend a secret. Her friend promised not to tell anyone. Later that day, Chelsea heard some other girls in her class talking about what she had told her friend. Chelsea felt disappointed and sad that her friend did not keep her promise.

It is disappointing and hurtful when someone does not keep a promise. Sometimes it makes it hard to trust that person the next time. The good news is that God never breaks any of the promises He makes in the Bible. He promised to send Jesus, and He did! God promises to forgive us of our sins when we trust in Jesus, and He does! It may take a long time for each and every promise to be fulfilled, but in the end every one of the good promises God makes will happen!

DIG DEEPER

Read about a few other promises God made in the Bible. Put a
star by the one below that means the most to you.

Exodus 14:14

Psalm 32:8

Isaiah 41:13

Romans 10:13

Philippians 4:19

James 1:5

PRAY

Read the verse you placed a star beside. Pray and
thank God for the promise He made in the verse.

34
TELL OTHERS

If you confess with your mouth, "Jesus is Lord," and believe in your heart that God raised him from the dead, you will be saved. One believes with the heart, resulting in righteousness, and one confesses with the mouth, resulting in salvation.—Romans 10:9–10

Most people think the word *confess* means that you admit to doing something wrong. Or you tell another person what you did wrong. That is one meaning of the word, but it is not exactly what God is talking about in Romans 10:9–10. In these verses, God is telling us it is important for us to confess or tell someone what we believe about Jesus and what He has done for us. When you confess your belief in Jesus, you are telling people that you believe He is God's Son, that He died on the cross to pay for your sins, and that He was buried and rose after three days. Confessing to what you believe lets others know that you have decided to follow Jesus and look forward to being with God forever.

DIG DEEPER

Make a list below of things you believe about Jesus and what He has done for you. Then make a list of people you can confess to or tell what you wrote. Plan to tell them what you believe this week!

What I Believe About Jesus

People I Can Tell

PRAY

Pray for the courage to tell others what you believe about Jesus. Thank Jesus for all the things He has done for you.

MAKING IT RIGHT

God presented him to demonstrate his righteousness at
the present time, so that he would be just and justify
the one who has faith in Jesus.—Romans 3:26

Evie asked her dad to buy her a pack of gum as they were going through the checkout line. "Not today," he replied. When he turned his head to place his items on the counter, Evie quickly grabbed the gum and placed it in her pocket. By the time they got home, Evie felt bad about taking the gum. She told her dad what she had done. Her father was disappointed. He told Evie she had to make things right by returning the gum to the store and asking the store manager to forgive her.

Being righteous means we are right with God based on His laws or standards. There is nothing we can do on our own to make ourselves right with God because we all sin. That's where Jesus comes in. Jesus is righteous because He lived without sin and kept all God's laws. The only way we can be made righteous or right with God is to believe in Jesus and the sacrifice He made for us.

DIG DEEPER

When we have accepted God's gift of salvation, the way we live changes. We want to do what is right and pleasing to God. What things do you need Jesus to make right for you?

_____

_____

_____

_____

_____

_____

_____

PRAY

Thank Jesus for doing for you what you could not do for yourself. Ask Him to give you the courage to want to do the things that please Him.

ARTIFACT CHECK

In the past few devotions, you have been reading about the message of the gospel. Jesus said, "It is finished," just before He died on the cross. Jesus meant that the price had been paid for our sins and He had done what God had sent Him to do. The word *gospel* actually means good news. You may be thinking that Jesus dying and then being placed in a grave with a stone rolled in front of it isn't good news. And you would be correct if that was the end of the story.

Archaeologists haven't found the actual stone that was rolled in front of Jesus' tomb, but they have made discoveries about stones like it. In Jesus' time, the poor were buried in nearby caves. Only the wealthy or rich could buy a tomb cut out of rock and a rolling stone for the opening. Most people just placed a square stone against the cave entrance. In the Bible, Matthew says that Joseph of Arimathea, a wealthy Jewish leader, allowed Jesus to be buried in his tomb, so it is likely that a round stone was placed in front of the grave. The Bible also says that the stone had been rolled away, which makes us believe Jesus' grave had a round stone and not a square stone.

Although archaeologists haven't found the actual gravestone used to close Jesus' tomb, they believe they have found the actual place where He was crucified and buried—the Church of the Holy Sepulchre. The church is as large as a football field and believed to cover the place in Golgotha were Jesus was crucified as well as the tomb of Joseph of Arimathea. The site has been identified as the place where Jesus was buried because of evidence discovered under the floor of the church. The fact that Jesus was crucified, buried, and rose from the dead is the good news of the gospel!

WHAT IS THE GOSPEL?

The gospel is the good news about who Jesus is and what He has done for us. It is about salvation and the kingdom of God. *Salvation* means saving us from punishment for our sins. It is something that only Jesus can do, and that is why we call Him our Savior.

God's plan is for His people to accept His gift of salvation. How can you do that? Read about God's plan below. Talk to a family member or a Christian adult at church if you have questions.

1. God Rules—The Bible tells us God created everything, including you and me. He is in charge of everything (Genesis 1:1; Colossians 1:16–17; Revelation 4:11).

2. We Sinned—We all choose to disobey God. The Bible calls this sin. Sin separates us from God and deserves God's punishment of death (Romans 3:23; 6:23).

3. God Provided—God sent Jesus, the perfect solution to our sin problem, to rescue us from the punishment we deserve. It's something we could never do on our own. Jesus alone saves us (John 3:16; Ephesians 2:8–9).

4. Jesus Gives—Jesus lived a perfect life, died on the cross for our sins, and rose again. Because Jesus gave up His life for us, we can be welcomed into God's family for eternity (Romans 5:8; 2 Corinthians 5:21; 1 Peter 3:18).

HOW DO WE RESPOND?

Jesus offers us the best gift ever. All we need to do is accept His gift. If you are ready to respond and accept the gift of salvation, just follow these steps (some people call these the ABCs of Becoming a Christian):

1. Admit—Tell God that you know you are a sinner. Tell Him you are sorry for doing your own thing and turning away from Him through your thoughts, words, and actions (Romans 3:23). Repent or turn away from your sin, and turn to Jesus, trusting only in Him to save you (Acts 3:19; 1 John 1:9).

2. Believe—Believe that Jesus is God's Son and receive His gift of forgiveness from sin. Believe that only Jesus can save you and you cannot save yourself from your sin problem. Place your trust in Jesus and what He did for you through His life, death, and resurrection (John 14:6; Acts 4:12; Acts 16:31; Ephesians 2:8–9).

3. Confess—Tell God and others what you believe. Jesus is not only your Savior; He is your Lord. That means Jesus is in charge and you are following Him and doing what He says in the Bible. You are born again into a new life and can look forward to being with God forever (Romans 10:9–10,13).

CATALOG YOUR FINDS

In the previous devotions you learned about God's plan for you and the gospel. Use these pages to catalog your finds. Check the box next to the statement that best applies to you.

☐ I want to discover more before I am ready to accept Jesus as my Savior and Lord.

☐ I am ready to accept Jesus as my Savior and Lord. I will talk to a Christian adult about my decision.

☐ I have already accepted Jesus as my Savior and Lord. I will continue to discover more about how to live as a follower of Him.

What questions do you have about being a
Christian or the Bible?

Write a prayer thanking God for the good
news about Jesus and His plan for you.

ARTIFACT CHECK

People sometimes wonder if the records of Jesus' trial in the Bible are really what happened. You can read about His trial in the Gospels (the first four books of the New Testament). One of the Gospels is the book of John. In chapter 18 you can read John's account of Jesus' trial. More than a hundred years ago, thousands of pieces of papyrus—a type of paper used back in Jesus' time—were found in a garbage pile in Egypt. When translators started going through the pieces, they found a piece with words from the Gospel of John written on it. The piece was less than nine centimeters high and six centimeters wide and it contained verses from John 18. If you are interested in knowing what the papyrus said, go to your Bible and read verses 31 to 33 and 37 to 38. Scholars believe this is probably the oldest copy of a part of the New Testament, and it shows that the Bible has not been changed even though it has been copied many times over thousands of years.

Archaeologists have made other finds that prove Jesus' trial was a real event and that the people mentioned as being part of the trial really existed. In the year 2000 a team started uncovering the site of a prison in Jerusalem. It took them ten years to uncover the entire site. As they uncovered the site, they found a sewage system that was part of Herod's palace—the place the wise men met Herod when they were searching for baby Jesus! It is also likely to be the spot where Jesus stood before Herod and was mocked before His crucifixion. Acts 4:27 mentions Herod, Pontius Pilate, the Gentiles, and the people of Israel gathering against Jesus in Jerusalem and putting Him on trial.

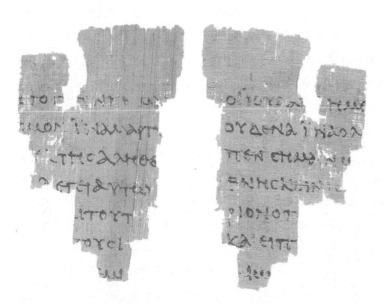

Papyrus pieces with words from the Gospel of John

CATALOG YOUR FINDS

Archaeologists often catalog their finds by placing them in grids or charts using symbols or pictures to group the items together. Read each of the verses below. Then catalog each verse under one of the images representing God's plan of salvation.

John 3:16	*Revelation 4:11*	*Romans 5:8*
1 Peter 3:18	*Romans 3:23*	*Genesis 1:1*
2 Corinthians 5:21	*Colossians 1:16–17*	*Romans 6:23*
Ephesians 2:8–9		

GOD RULES   **WE SINNED**   **GOD PROVIDED**   **JESUS GIVES**

_____ _____ _____ _____

_____ _____ _____

_____ _____

Note: You can check your answers on page 208.

WE RESPOND

The last part of God's plan is our response. We can use the ABCs of becoming a Christian as a tool to help us remember how to respond. Read each of the verses below. Then catalog each verse under the correct heading.

Romans 10:9–10	*Romans 3:23*	*Acts 4:12*
1 John 1:9	*Romans 10:13*	*John 14:6*
John 1:11–13	*Romans 6:23*	*Romans 5:8*
Acts 3:19		

Admit you are a sinner

Believe Jesus is God's Son and accept his gift of forgiveness

---

Confess your faith in Jesus

Note: You can check your answers on page 208.

A NEW CREATION

Therefore, if anyone is in Christ, he is a new creation; the old has passed away, and see, the new has come!—2 Corinthians 5:17

Becca and her mom loved to go to yard sales to find old things to fix up. They would buy an old, worn-out piece of furniture and give it new life. Becca and her mom would clean up the piece, sand it, and repaint it until the old outside shone like new.

When you become a Christian, you become a new creation in Christ. People may not see a difference in how you look on the outside, but they can see the difference in how you act and respond to difficult situations. Maybe you respond with kind words when someone is being mean to you, or instead of trying to get back at him you decide to forgive him. When you decide to follow Jesus, you no longer think and act the same way. Jesus makes your life shiny and new!

DIG DEEPER

Use the space to draw a picture of something old and worn out. Then draw a picture of how it would look when it has been restored or made new.

PRAY

Praise Jesus for making you a new creation. Thank Him for changing the way you live and how you treat others.

FRUIT OF THE SPIRIT

But the fruit of the Spirit is love, joy, peace, patience, kindness, goodness, faithfulness, gentleness, and self-control. The law is not against such things.—Galatians 5:22–23

Who is your favorite superhero? What makes him or her a superhero? Maybe it's the special powers he has or because she lives and acts differently than regular people. Superheroes are fun to read about or watch in movies. They often have unique powers they use to sweep in and save the day. However, we all know that superheroes and their powers aren't real.

But did you know you have superpowers if you believe in Jesus? You do, and you have more than one! In Galatians we read about the fruit of the Spirit. The fruit of the Spirit describes actions or characteristics of a Christian. These things help us live and act differently than the person who doesn't follow Jesus. So take your superpowers and go out and show the world how to live like Jesus!

DIG DEEPER

Memorize the fruit of the Spirit below. Circle the one or ones most difficult for you to demonstrate.

LOVE JOY *Patience*
PEACE KINDNESS
GOODNESS FAITHFULNESS
Self-control *Gentleness*

PRAY

Pray that God will help you have the strength to demonstrate the fruit of the Spirit in how you live every day. Ask Him to help you with the ones you struggle with.

LET YOUR LIGHT SHINE

In the same way, let your light shine before others,
so that they may see your good works and give
glory to your Father in heaven.—Matthew 5:16

Have you ever experienced a darkness so dark that you could not even see your hand in front of your face? How did you feel? It can be scary and frightening when you are stuck in the dark. It can be impossible to see the right way to go or the things that block your way. But then someone turns on a flashlight or a night-light, and the darkness is immediately gone. Darkness is the absence of light, so when you turn on even the smallest light in a dark place, it brings light to the entire place. You can see the right way to go, and you know you won't trip over anything that blocks your path.

The Bible often refers to sin as darkness and not obeying God, and Jesus is referred to as the light or truth. When Jesus says, "Let your light shine," He is asking you to show people around you what it means to follow Him and do the things He asks. It may mean that you love others the way Jesus did or that you are kind to someone no one else likes or you give up your place in line to let someone else be first. Jesus wants you to be the light that shows others how to follow Him.

DIG DEEPER

Beneath the drawings of the flashlight, light bulb and lighthouse write the purpose of each item.

How can you be the light of Jesus in your school, home, or neighborhood? Write your responses below.

_____

_____

_____

PRAY

Being the light isn't always easy, especially when it means giving up something. Pray that God will help you show others that Jesus loves them and they can know the truth about Him.

BE A GOD-PLEASER

Peter and the apostles replied, "We must obey
God rather than people."—Acts 5:29

Kimmie's friends kept pressuring her to go with them to see a
movie her parents didn't want her to see. They told her it would
be okay to tell her parents she was going to see a different movie
but then sneak into the one they wanted her to see. Kimmie didn't
feel good about not being honest with her parents, but she didn't
want her friends to think she was a baby for not going with them.
Instead of standing up and doing what would please God, Kimmie
decided to do what her friends wanted.

In Acts 5, Peter and the apostles (followers of Jesus) had to
decide if they were going to please God or the high priest. The
high priest didn't want them teaching people about Jesus. The
high priest had even placed Peter and his friends in prison for
doing so. But they decided that instead of pleasing people they
would do what pleased God. Peter and his friends knew it was
more important to obey God even if it meant going back to prison.

DIG DEEPER

Read the whole story about Peter and his friends in Acts 5:12–32. Being a people-pleaser instead of a God-pleaser can lead you to make poor choices. Make a list of things you can say when people want you to do what pleases them and not God.

40

DOING WHAT IS GOOD

Mankind, he has told each of you what is good and what it is the LORD requires of you: to act justly, to love faithfulness, and to walk humbly with your God.—Micah 6:8

Do you ever wonder how God wants you to live? Do you wonder what it means to live a good life? In Micah 6:8, the prophet Micah tells us exactly what is good and what is needed to live a good life according to God. It's basically just three things that seem small but are really huge. First, act justly. This means you treat others fairly and with respect. Second, you love faithfulness. Loving faithfulness means you stay close to God, you love the things He loves, learn more about His ways, and pray or talk to Him every day. Then, you walk humbly with God. This means you don't brag about yourself and what you have done. You brag about God because everything comes from Him. In other words, you give Him all the credit. That's it—just three not-so-small ways to do what pleases God.

DIG DEEPER

Write examples of how you might follow each step to doing good.

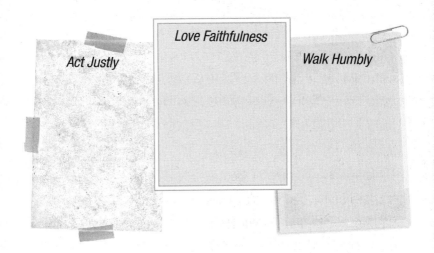

Act Justly

Love Faithfulness

Walk Humbly

PRAY

Thank God for telling us exactly what He requires us to do. Ask Him to help you do what He has required.

A KING AFTER GOD'S OWN HEART

After removing him, he raised up David as their
king and testified about him, "I have found David
the son of Jesse to be a man after my own heart,
who will carry out all my will."—Acts 13:22

It wasn't the first time Brett had messed up, but this time he really did it! Brett had lied to his parents about his grades. He knew if he told them he was failing math, they wouldn't let him go to his friend's birthday party. Report cards came home on Thursday, and the party wasn't until Friday. Brett decided to hide his report card. His parents found his report card under a book on the desk in the hall. Now Bret was not only in trouble for lying, but he was also in trouble for trying to cover up his lie.

The Bible tells us about King David and some of the times he really messed up. Even though King David messed up and broke God's law, he was called a man after God's own heart. David was a king and had lots of power over people, but he also knew that he was not above God and God's laws. When King David broke one of God's laws, he repented or asked God to forgive him. King David not only asked God to forgive him, but he also asked God to help him change and do what would please Him. This is what it means to be a man after God's own heart.

DIG DEEPER

David wrote many of the Psalms as prayers to God, admitting his mistakes and asking God to forgive him. Here are a few you can read to learn how to be a person after God's own heart.

Psalm 32
Psalm 51
Psalm 130

PRAY

The next time you mess up, pray, and ask God to forgive you. Ask Him to help you turn away from doing what is wrong and do what pleases Him instead.

ARTIFACT CHECK

King David ruled Israel for nearly forty years and may be one of their most famous kings. He was known for killing a lion and a bear to protect his sheep, he defeated a giant named Goliath, and he brought the Ten Commandments into Jerusalem. Even though David was so famous, and a lot was written about him in the Bible, archaeologists did not find any evidence about him until 1993. In the ancient city of Dan, archaeologists found a piece of stone slab they called the Tel-Dan Inscription. The slab is the first historical evidence found about King David. The inscription talks about a victory by an Aramean king over the House of David. This find proved that King David was not a made-up character in the Bible and that his enemies still recognized him as the founder of the kingdom of Judah.

The Tel-Dan Inscription

The Royal Seal of Hezekiah (bulla)

King David was not the only king who followed God. The Bible tells us that King Hezekiah also followed God's ways and tried to lead his people to do what God required. You can read about him in 2 Chronicles 32. The Royal Seal of Hezekiah or *bulla* that was used to seal documents shut was found in 2015. The bulla was an important find because it was the first bulla of an Israelite king to be found on an official dig site. The bulla is one-centimeter around, which is about the size of the top of a pencil or highlighter. On the bulla there is a two-winged sun disk and ankh symbols which read, "Belonging to Hezekiah." The seal was found in a trash dump near a royal building that was dated to be in use in King Hezekiah's day.

NO GRUMBLING

Do everything without grumbling and
arguing.—Philippians 2:14

It's too hot. I'm tired. No one else's mom makes them help with the laundry." The list of complaints went on and on. Taylor and Reese didn't want to help their mother with the household chores. With every chore they did, they grumbled and argued all the way until the task was complete. Their mom was tired of hearing all the complaining and arguing. She sat the girls down and explained that as part of the family, they had to help around the house. She pulled out her Bible and read Philippians 2:14 to the girls and explained that to please Jesus, they needed to work without grumbling or arguing. Taylor and Reese told their mom they were sorry for their attitudes and promised to help finish the chores with a better attitude. The girls soon discovered that when they didn't stop to complain, the work was quicker and they had more time to go out and play.

DIG DEEPER

Write Philippians 2:14 below and then on several sticky notes too. Place the notes in areas where you do tasks that might lead you to grumble or complain. Each time you are tempted to grumble, stop and repeat the verse aloud to reset your way of thinking.

_____

_____

_____

_____

_____

_____

_____

PRAY

Ask God to forgive you for the times you have grumbled and complained about completing a task. Ask Him to help you honor Him by doing everything with a cheerful heart.

EVERYTHING YOU DO

Whatever you do, do it from the heart, as something done for the Lord and not for people, knowing that you will receive the reward of an inheritance from the Lord. You serve the Lord Christ.—Colossians 3:23–24

Samantha agreed to rake leaves for her neighbor, Mr. Jenkins. She arrived early Saturday morning to get started on the job, and Mr. Jenkins sat on the porch to supervise. Every time Samantha missed a leaf or hit one of the flowerbeds with the rake, Mr. Jenkins would complain. At lunch, Samantha went home for a break. She told her dad how she didn't want to go back and finish because she couldn't please Mr. Jenkins. Her dad said she needed to think of herself raking leaves for Jesus and not Mr. Jenkins. "If you were doing the job for Jesus, would you want to do your best and finish what you started?" he asked. "Jesus sees everything we do, and we should do everything as if it's for Him because in the end it really is."

Samantha decided to go back and finish the job. She wanted to do her best because it mattered to Jesus. Samantha even decided to go the extra step and pick up the limbs that had fallen in the yard because that would please Jesus!

DIG DEEPER

Another verse that tells us how to do our work is Colossians 3:17. Read the verse. Then make a list of things that are hard for you to do. Write how you might do those things as if you were doing them for the Lord.

Things That Are Hard to Do:

_____

_____

How I Can Do Them for the Lord:

_____

_____

PRAY

Ask God to help you do everything you do in a way that pleases Him.

THINK ABOUT IT

Finally brothers and sisters, whatever is true, whatever is honorable, whatever is just, whatever is pure, whatever is lovely, whatever is commendable—if there is any moral excellence and if there is anything praiseworthy—dwell on these things.—Philippians 4:8

Jamal loves playing video games with his friends. One of the games they like to play has a lot of bad language and violence. He told his mom it was no big deal because the game isn't real, and it's not like he would talk or act like the characters on the game. But one day when he got angry, Jamal said a bad word he had heard on the game.

Even though it may not seem like a big deal, little things that you let into your mind will change how you think and act. That is why Paul encouraged the church in Philippi not just to think on but also dwell on things that are true, honorable, just, pure, lovely, commendable, and praiseworthy. He knew what we put into our minds eventually shows up in our lives. When you dwell on something, that means you think about it and talk about it over and over again for a long time. If you want good things to come out, you need to put good things in. God wants you to spend your time dwelling on the things that please Him.

DIG DEEPER

Before you start a new game, movie, or book, ask yourself if it fits the definition of being *true*, *honorable*, *pure*, *lovely*, *just*, *excellent*, *commendable*, and *praiseworthy*. Find and circle each of these words in the puzzle.

```
L  H  O  N  O  R  A  B  L  E  L  I  G  J  U  S  T
O  O  A  S  W  S  S  P  L  A  N  T  S  I  O  P  L
V  N  B  D  E  T  C  O  M  M  E  N  D  A  B  L  E
E  E  X  C  E  L  L  E  N  T  K  U  B  H  F  R  L
L  S  G  R  D  P  R  A  I  S  E  W  O  R  T  H  Y
Y  T  R  U  E  I  B  I  R  D  S  U  P  U  R  E  N
```

Note: You can check your answers on page 208.

PRAY

Ask God to help you dwell on the things that please Him.

WHOLESOME TALK

Do not let any unwholesome talk come out of
your mouths, but only what is helpful for building
others up according to their needs, that it may
benefit those who listen.—Ephesians 4:29 NIV

Has anybody ever told you that if you don't have something nice to say, don't say anything at all? It really is good advice and goes right along with Ephesians 4:29. Sometimes we all let unwholesome talk come out of our mouths, and that doesn't just mean we say a bad word. Unwholesome talk is anything that is not true, is hurtful to another person, or puts someone else down. At one time or another someone has said something mean to you or something untrue about you. Think about how that made you feel. Chances are it hurt deep down inside even if you tried not to show it on the outside. Words really do hurt!

In Ephesians, Paul was telling the people who were part of the church in Ephesus that they needed to be careful about the words they used. Paul wanted them to talk to each other in ways that were helpful, kind, and truthful. He knew that speaking to people in this way encourages them. Paul also knew those who didn't believe in Jesus were listening to what believers said to one another. So be careful with your words and use them to build each other up.

DIG DEEPER

Read and memorize Psalm 141:3. Before you speak, ask yourself:

Are my words kind?	☐ yes	☐ no
Are my words helpful?	☐ yes	☐ no
Are my words true?	☐ yes	☐ no

If you can answer yes to all three questions, then go ahead and speak up.

PRAY

Recite Psalm 141:3 as a prayer whenever you are tempted to speak any words that will not be helpful to others.

LOVE WHO?

But I say to you who listen: Love your enemies, do what is good to those who hate you, bless those who curse you, pray for those who mistreat you.—Luke 6:27–28

Michael didn't want to go to school. He wanted to stay home and watch TV in his room all day. When his mom asked what was going on at school, Michael told her about Alex, the class bully. Alex was bigger and meaner than everyone else in the fourth grade. He threatened to beat people up over nothing, he called them stupid, and he always tried to get his way. Michael told his mom he was just tired of dealing with Alex.

Michael's mom told him everybody deals with bullies in their lives. She told Michael she was proud of him for telling her. She read Luke 6:27–28 to him and told him he didn't have to like what Alex was doing, but he had to love and pray for him. His mom explained that Jesus wants us to love and pray for our enemies because they are sinners just like us. However, we do not have to love the sin because sin is the reason Jesus had to go to the cross. His mom told Michael she would help him deal with what was happening. She suggested that they start by praying for Alex.

DIG DEEPER

Inside the heart, write the initials of people who are hard for you to love.

Love Who?

PRAY

Pray for the people whose initials you wrote in the heart. Ask God to help you love them and treat them with kindness even when they mistreat you.

ARTIFACT CHECK

Did you know that people in the Bible had to deal with bullies too? It's true. Sanballat was one. You can read all about him in Nehemiah 2 and 4. Sanballat bullied Nehemiah and the Israelite people when they tried to rebuild the walls of Jerusalem. He made fun of Nehemiah, spread lies about him, and tried to distract him from work. Sanballat even planned to hurt Nehemiah and the people who were working on the wall. Because he was the governor of Samaria, Sanballat had a lot of power. Holding this position made it easy for him to get other people to help him bully Nehemiah and the Israelites.

Around 1909, Egyptian farmers found one hundred and seventy-five documents in the city of Elephantine. The documents, called the Elephantine papyri, record a lot of the details found in Nehemiah. They date from 495 BC to 399 BC, which happens to

be the time when Sanballat lived. One of the documents known as the Elephantine Temple Papyrus mentions that Delaiah and Shelemiah, sons of Sanballat, governor of Samaria, sent him a letter about the rebuilding of the wall. This is proof that Sanballat was a real person and was who the Bible said he was.

BE HOLY

> But as the one who called you is holy, you also are to be holy in all your conduct; for it is written, Be holy, because I am holy.—1 Peter 1:15–16

Being holy sounds like a really hard thing to do. And what does it even mean to be holy? When God calls us to be holy, He is talking about being set apart and different from the world. God's not telling us we must be perfect, because He knows we can't be—only Jesus was perfect. God wants us to be more like Jesus, learn to hate what is evil, and try to live a life that pleases Him.

Remember a few devotions back you read about Kimmie and her decision to follow her friends in doing something that was wrong? That is an example of not being holy. A person who is trying to be holy in her conduct or actions would not be part of ungodly plans. Instead a person who is trying to be holy would make her choice to be different or set apart. Even though it sounds tough to be different and set apart, the good news is you are not alone. God has sent the Holy Spirit to help you.

DIG DEEPER

Read these verses to help you understand a little more about the Holy Spirit and how He works in your life. Make a few notes about what you learn.

John 14:26

John 16:13

Romans 8:26

1 Corinthians 3:16

PRAY

Ask God to help you be holy and live a life that pleases Him.

LOVE ONE ANOTHER

This is my command: Love one another
as I have loved you.—John 15:12

"I love ice cream and tacos and grape soda." "I really love, love, love soccer!" Have you ever noticed just how many times people use the word *love* to describe something they like? Or how many times people say, "I love you," out of habit? Love is more than liking someone or something. Love is an action, not a feeling. In John 15:12, Jesus is commanding us to love one another as He loved us. Notice that the word *love* here is something we must do. Jesus is telling us we must take the action of showing love to others. Remember how He did that? Jesus showed love to people who sinned, who didn't love Him, and who other people looked down on.

Jesus wants you to do the same—to show love to other people the way He shows love to you. That might mean helping someone everyone else would turn their back on or eating lunch with the kid everyone else thinks isn't cool. Think about how you can put love into action and not just into words!

DIG DEEPER

In 1 Corinthians 13, love is described in some of the ways listed below. Give yourself a letter grade to describe how you demonstrate each description. A would be the best and F would mean you need to work on it.

LOVE	MY GRADE
Love is patient.	_____
Love is kind.	_____
Love does not want what others have.	_____
Love is not selfish.	_____
Love is not rude.	_____
Love does not keep a record of wrong.	_____
Love rejoices in truth.	_____

PRAY

Read back over the grades you gave yourself. Ask God to help you in any of the areas where you gave yourself a failing or low grade.

SERVE OTHERS

Sitting down, he called the Twelve and said
to them, "If anyone wants to be first, he must
be last and servant of all."—Mark 9:35

Chloe didn't understand how someone who wants to be first must be last. And then he must be a servant to all? That all sounded backwards. Her teacher explained that when Jesus made this statement in Mark 9:35, He was talking to His disciples. Jesus' disciples were arguing about which of them was the greatest. The disciples were trying to decide who would be the greatest based on things they had done. Jesus wanted them to know that in God's kingdom, success and being great is not measured by how much you do or how much you own. In God's kingdom, those who put others first before themselves and serve others are considered the greatest. If you want to be the greatest in God's kingdom, put others first. Be humble and be a servant who cares for the needs of others. In other words, put the importance on others and not yourself!

DIG DEEPER

What can you do to serve others this week? List a few ideas in the space below.

_____

_____

_____

_____

_____

_____

_____

_____

PRAY

Ask God to give you opportunities to serve others and put them first. Ask God to forgive you for the times you tried to put yourself first.

NO FEAR

For God has not given us a spirit of fear, but one of power, love, and sound judgment.—2 Timothy 1:7

Sarah didn't want to give her book report aloud to her class. She was afraid to stand up in front of a group of people and talk. Just thinking about it made her stomach hurt and her hands sweat. Her mom tried to encourage her. She suggested that Sarah practice at home in front of her family. Or that Sarah could look over everyone's heads to the back wall while she was talking. Nothing her mom suggested seemed to make Sarah feel better.

Everyone is afraid of something. Maybe it's the dark or spiders or monsters under the bed. God doesn't want you to let your fears keep you from doing the things He has planned for you. He wants you to trust Him to help you do the things He asks you to do. The good news is that God has given you what you need so you don't have to live in fear.

DIG DEEPER

What are some things that make you fearful? List them below.

1.

2.

3.

PRAY

Spend time praying about the fears you listed. Thank God that He is bigger and stronger than all your fears.

PEACE

If possible, as far as it depends on you, live at
peace with everyone.—Romans 12:18

Living at peace with everyone is not always easy. There's your
brother or sister who takes your things and starts arguments with
you every day. There's that kid at school who keeps bugging you
to give him the answers on your homework. Then there's the kid
on your basketball team who wants to argue about whose fault it
is when the team loses. So you go home and turn on the TV, and
the characters on your favorite show are yelling at one another.

The Bible says to live at peace with everyone as much as possible. How are you supposed to do that? Part of the verse says,
"as far as it depends on you." That means we should look and
see if we are at fault and be willing to apologize for our part in the
conflict. It also means we should be willing to forgive and make
things right if we can. The verse also says, "if possible." Jesus
knows it may not always be possible to have peace. But He wants
you to do all you can to make peace happen.

DIG DEEPER

In Genesis 26:12–33, the land in which Isaac lived was dry, and it was hard to find water. Arguments arose over the wells in the region. Read the passage to see how Isaac restored peace. Think about someone you think is hard to live at peace with. Make a few notes about what you can do to make peace with that person.

_____

_____

_____

_____

_____

PRAY

The next time you find yourself in conflict, ask God to help you make peace and forgive the other person.

AVOID TEMPTATION

Therefore, submit to God. Resist the devil,
and he will flee from you.—James 4:7

Dylan's grandmother made homemade cookies. She told Dylan
he could have one but not until after dinner. Dylan didn't know if
he could wait for two hours. The smell of the cookies hung in the
air. Every time he walked through the kitchen, he saw them cool-
ing on the counter. Soon the only thing Dylan could think about
was the cookies. He started thinking it wouldn't hurt to just eat
the smallest one; surely nobody would notice. Dylan knew he was
getting close to giving into his temptation. He knew he needed to
go outside and play until dinner so he would not give in.

Jesus faced temptation too. The difference between us and
Jesus is that every single time, Jesus resisted the temptation. It's
hard not to give in when we think it won't hurt anyone or when
everyone else tells us it's okay. It's not. Once we give in to the
small temptations, it doesn't take long to start giving into bigger
ones. Follow Jesus' and Dylan's example. When you are tempted,
flee from the temptation.

DIG DEEPER

Read about how Jesus avoided temptation in Matthew 4:1–11. Think about tempting situations you face and how you can run from them. A few ideas for following Jesus' example are listed to get you started.

Hide the Word in your heart.—Psalm 119:11

Love Jesus more than anything and keep His commands.
        —John 14:15

Remember the battle is already won.—Philippians 1:6

PRAY

When you face temptation remember God has given you the ability to have control over any temptation. Ask God to help you make the choice to avoid temptation and follow Jesus' example.

FORGIVE ONE ANOTHER

And be kind and compassionate to one another, forgiving one another, just as God also forgave you in Christ.—Ephesians 4:32

Sydney didn't want to forgive her brother. He read her diary and told his friends what she wrote about a boy in her class. His friends were teasing her constantly. Sydney's brother didn't even feel sorry for what he had done. Sydney thought about all the things she could do to get back at him. Sydney said she would never forgive him or talk to him again. But that's when her mom stepped in and reminded her that God said we should forgive others because He has forgiven us.

Think about how many times God has forgiven you for things you have done. God forgives you (and everyone who believes in Jesus) every single time you mess up. God not only forgives you, but He asks you to forgive others. Part of forgiving others is not trying to get back at them, not wishing bad things will happen to them, and not being happy when something bad does happen. Forgiving means letting go of your desire to get back at the person who hurt you and wishing them well instead.

DIG DEEPER

Read the parable or story of the unforgiving servant in Matthew 18:21–35. Jesus used parables to teach lessons to people. What do you think He wanted people to learn from this parable? Write your answer below.

_____

_____

_____

_____

_____

_____

_____

PRAY

Forgiving others who hurt you is hard. Ask God to help you forgive and thank Him for forgiving you.

54

BE CONTENT

He then told them, "Watch out and be on guard against all greed, because one's life is not in the abundance of his possessions."—Luke 12:15

If someone gave you a hundred dollars, what would you buy? Would you spend it all on yourself? Or would you share it with others? Would you spend it all and still want more? The world tells us we should try to get as much stuff as we can to be happy or content. But what usually happens once you get the latest video game? A new one comes out and then you want it too. The thing you bought that you thought would make you happy now sits in the back of your closet unused with more stuff piling on top of it.

Being satisfied with what we have is what it means to be content. When you are content, you know that your stuff—or how much of it you have—is not what's important. Greed is the opposite of being content with what you have. Greed makes you think and focus more on what you want than on God. He doesn't want us to become greedy and just pile up more and more stuff. God wants us to focus more on Him than on our stuff.

DIG DEEPER

Proverbs has a lot to say about greed. Read each verse below and note what it says about being greedy.

Proverbs 15:27

Proverbs 22:1

Proverbs 22:9

Proverbs 28:22

Proverbs 28:25

PRAY

Ask God to help you be content with what you have and not want more than you need. When you feel tempted to act greedy, pray one of the verses from Proverbs to act against your temptation.

PRAY CONSTANTLY

Pray constantly.—1 Thessalonians 5:17

Katie's grandmother had a special closet in her house she called her prayer closet. Every morning, her grandmother would take her Bible and go in the closet to pray. But Katie's grandmother didn't stop praying when she left the closet. Katie would hear her grandmother say a short prayer when she was driving, when she was cooking dinner, or even when she was out weeding the garden. It seemed to Katie that her grandmother was constantly praying.

Praying constantly doesn't mean you have to be in your room with your head bowed and eyes closed all day. It means you talk to God throughout the day just like Katie's grandmother did. God tells us to pray constantly in 1 Thessalonians 5:17 and to pray about everything in Philippians 4:6. So if He wants us to pray constantly and about everything, that means He wants to hear from us all day every day.

DIG DEEPER

Use some of the ideas below to help you start a habit of praying constantly.

- Pray as you do your chores. If you are folding laundry, pray for the person whose clothing you are folding.
- When you see something you are thankful for, stop and praise God.
- Talk to God like you would a friend. You don't need any fancy words.
- Pray while you wait in line at school, baseball practice, or at a restaurant.
- Sing a praise song as a prayer.

Can you think of other ways to pray constantly?

PRAY

Thank God that He never grows tired of listening to you pray. Ask Him to help you make a habit of praying constantly.

FOLLOW HIS EXAMPLE

Therefore, be imitators of God, as dearly
loved children.—Ephesians 5:1

Have you ever told someone you want to be just like them when you grow up? Maybe it was a parent, teacher, or neighbor. When we want to be like someone, we often imitate or copy the things he or she does. We spend time with the person and learn how he thinks and acts. Then we try to do things the same way. Maybe it's dressing like that person dresses or trying to talk like she does, or maybe we like the things he likes. This kind of imitation can be a good thing if the person believes in Jesus and follows Him.

God wants us to be imitators of Him. He wants us to spend time with Him, learning to love the things He loves and treat people the way He treats them. When we imitate God, we are showing the world that we are His children and what a great Father He is!

DIG DEEPER

The Bible describes many characteristics of God. A few are listed below. How can you imitate those characteristics in your life?

TRUSTWORTHY

GOOD

FAITHFUL

LOVING HUMBLE

Caring

HONEST **Generous**

PRAY

Ask God to help you learn more about Him so you can be more like Him in the things you do.

CONTINUE GROWING

We haven't stopped praying for you. We are asking
that you may be filled with the knowledge of his will
in all wisdom and spiritual understanding, so that
you may walk worthy of the Lord . . . and growing
in the knowledge of God.—Colossians 1:9–10

Each year you grow a little taller, a little stronger, and a little smarter. To keep growing, you have to eat the right things, exercise, and get plenty of rest. If you want to grow smarter, you should keep reading, keep studying, and keep practicing. When you don't continue to take these steps, your body and mind can become weak.

As important as it is for your body and mind to continue to grow, it is more important for you to grow spiritually in your heart and soul. Growing in wisdom and spiritual understanding means you need to keep taking steps to make you closer to God and strengthen your trust in Him. That means you need to keep reading your Bible, keep praying, keep meeting with other believers, and keep asking questions. God wants you to continue growing in every way so you can please Him and do the good things He has planned for you.

DIG DEEPER

When you lift weights, you are strengthening your arm muscles. To see any effects, you must repeat the same exercise over and over. What are some exercises or habits you can repeat over and over to help you grow in your knowledge of God? List a few exercises and plan to start doing them today.

PRAY

Thank God for all the good things He has planned for you to do. Ask Him to help you continue to grow strong in your knowledge of Him.

58

BE GRATEFUL

My soul, bless the Lord, and do not forget all his benefits.
He forgives all your iniquity; he heals all your diseases.
He redeems your life from the Pit; he crowns you with
faithful love and compassion.—Psalm 103:2–4

Kayla's teacher assigned the class a writing assignment. She gave everyone a blank journal and asked them to write down something they were thankful for each day for the next week. The students were then to write a poem or short paragraph explaining each thing they wrote down. Kayla thought the assignment was going to be hard. Her family didn't have a lot of money or a big house. She didn't have all the brand-new things her friends had. But as Kayla started looking around her, she found that she had a lot to be grateful for. She had food to eat every day, she had a great big backyard to play in, and she had a bike to ride. Most importantly, Kayla realized she was grateful that Jesus forgives her sins and that she will one day live in heaven with Him.

DIG DEEPER

In the space below, make a list of the great things God has done for you.

_____

_____

_____

_____

_____

_____

_____

_____

PRAY

Praise God for each thing on your list. Thank Him for the things He has done and will continue to do for you.

CATALOG YOUR FINDS

In the previous devotions you have discovered how to live as a follower of Jesus. Use these two pages to catalog your finds. Answer the questions, and add any notes or drawings that will remind you of how Jesus wants you to live.

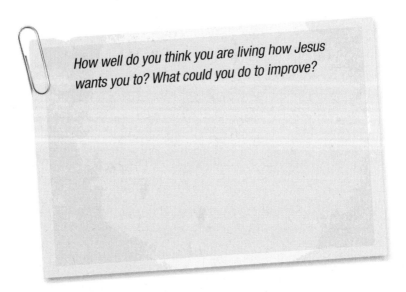

How well do you think you are living how Jesus wants you to? What could you do to improve?

Of the verses you read on pages 126–148, which do you think is the easiest for you to follow? Which verse is the hardest for you to follow?

Part of living the way Jesus wants you to live is knowing what the Bible says. What verse from pages 126–148 will you commit to memorizing?

TELLING OTHERS ABOUT JESUS

Declare his glory among the nations, his wondrous
works among all peoples.—Psalm 96:3

In the next few devotions, you will discover new things to help
you tell others what you believe about Jesus and help them learn
how they can trust Jesus too. People need to hear the good news
about how God loves them and sent Jesus to die for their sins so
that they can be made right with Him and live with Him forever.
But sometimes we don't tell others because we are afraid they
will make fun of us or that they will no longer want to be our
friend. It might sound scary, but don't worry. God will help you.

DIG DEEPER

Here are a few tips to help you talk to others about Jesus.

1. Think about someone on your soccer team or at school who needs to hear the good news.
2. Find something you have in common with that person. Get to know him and let him get to know you.
3. Ask him about the things he is having a hard time with. Offer to help. Listen and tell him you will be his friend.
4. Ask him about his church and beliefs. Listen to what he says, and share what you believe and why.
5. Invite him to church to learn more about Jesus.

PRAY

Ask God to help you tell people about Jesus. Pray that He will help you know what to say.

TWO ARE BETTER THAN ONE

Two are better than one because they have a good reward for their efforts. For if either falls, his companion can lift him up.—Ecclesiastes 4:9–10

Solomon became king when his father, David, died. We have already read about how David was a man after God's own heart. When Solomon became king, at first he followed his father's example. Once Solomon prayed and asked God for wisdom because he was just a youth who didn't have much experience in leading people. God was pleased that Solomon didn't ask for money, fame, long life, or selfish things that would just make him look good. God granted Solomon wisdom that no one before or after him has ever had.

Solomon later wrote the book of Ecclesiastes where today's verses are found. He recognized the wisdom of joining efforts or finding a friend who will stand with you. When you team up with someone, you can help and support one another. If Solomon, the wisest person who ever lived, thinks two are better than one, then maybe it's good advice to live by. Remember Solomon's words when you want to talk to someone about Jesus. Take a friend along with you. Remember, two are better than one!

DIG DEEPER

Having a friend who believes in Jesus the same way you do and who is willing to stand with you can give you courage to tell others about Him. Think about what qualities you look for in a friend. List those qualities in the space below.

_____

_____

_____

_____

_____

_____

_____

PRAY

Thank God for the wise words Solomon wrote in the Bible. Ask God to help you find friends who will stand with you and help you share the good news about Jesus.

I AM ONLY A YOUTH

Do not say, "I am only a youth," for you will go to everyone I send you to and speak whatever I tell you. Do not be afraid of anyone, for I will be with you to rescue you. This is the Lord's declaration.—Jeremiah 1:7–8

Alex's coach was telling the team about how the world began. But Alex knew the coach's ideas were wrong. She knew that the Bible teaches that God created everything and that many scientific facts prove what the Bible says is true. Alex wanted to speak up and say something, but she was afraid because she was just a kid and her coach was an adult. If only her mom were there to help her speak up and know what to say.

Jeremiah was one of God's prophets (someone who delivers God's message). When God chose Jeremiah to do this special job, Jeremiah said, "Oh no, Lord God! Look, I don't know how to speak since I am only a youth." Jeremiah wasn't sure he could do what God wanted him to. Our verses for today are God's reply to Jeremiah. Notice that God basically said, "It doesn't matter that you are young, because I will tell you what to say. Don't be afraid." God is still in charge, and He will give you the words to say and the courage to speak them just as He did for Jeremiah.

DIG DEEPER

You can read more about Jeremiah in the book of Jeremiah in the Old Testament. Even though you are young, God wants you to speak up and tell others what is true. Write three things you know are true that you can tell others.

1.

2.

3.

PRAY

Ask God to help you speak up and not be afraid. Pray that He will give you the words to say.

PUT ON YOUR FULL ARMOR

Take up the full armor of God, so that you may be able to resist in the evil day. . . . Stand, therefore, with truth like a belt around your waist, righteousness like armor on your chest, and your feet sandaled with readiness for the gospel of peace. In every situation take up the shield of faith with which you can extinguish all the flaming arrows of the evil one. Take the helmet of salvation and the sword of the Spirit—which is the word of God.—Ephesians 6:13–17

When you get up in the morning, what is one of the first things you do? Perhaps you brush your teeth or get dressed for the day. What clothes do you put on? It's important that you choose clothes that are right for the weather, the place you are going, and the things you will be doing. If you are going to school, you don't want to put on your full football uniform. If you are going to soccer practice, you definitely don't put on a fancy dress.

In Ephesians 6, Paul tells us we need to put on the full armor of God every day. Now this doesn't mean you put on actual armor. Paul is using the image of armor worn by a Roman soldier in his day. Each piece of armor was designed to protect the soldier in a specific way. For us to stand up against Satan and sin and to speak up for what is true about Jesus, we must be protected and prepared.

DIG DEEPER

Challenge yourself to memorize each piece of armor.

- **Belt of Truth**—Know and speak the truth.
- **Breastplate of Righteousness**—Protect your heart from evil thoughts and actions.
- **Sandals of Readiness for the Gospel**—Be ready to take the good news to others.
- **Shield of Faith**—Join shields with other Christians for protection and stand together.
- **Helmet of Salvation**—Protect your mind from ungodly thoughts.
- **Sword of the Spirit**—Memorize scriptures to stay sharp in understanding the Spirit's leading.

PRAY

As you pray, mention each piece of armor and ask God to make you ready to stand and speak up for the truth. Ask Him to help you make wise choices and be ready to share the good news with people you meet.

MAKE THE MOST OF EVERY OPPORTUNITY

Pay careful attention, then, to how you walk—not as unwise people but as wise—making the most of the time, because the days are evil.—Ephesians 5:15–16

Joshua didn't know if he really believed all the things his friend Toby said about Jesus. Toby told Joshua he believed in Jesus and wanted to be like Jesus, but many times Toby didn't act any different than other people. Toby would lie if it would get him out of trouble. He would talk about other people and call them names. And when others needed help, Toby didn't lend a hand.

God does not want us to waste the time He has given us or to miss the opportunities to show others what we believe. Ephesians 5:15 tells us to pay careful attention to how we walk. Other people are watching our actions. When people hear us say one thing but then act in another way, it confuses them. They aren't sure if we really mean it when we tell them we believe in Jesus or that Jesus is really who the Bible says He is. We also need to use the time God gives us wisely. We will not live forever, so we need to take advantage of the time we have to make sure people know about Jesus.

DIG DEEPER

Around the clock, record the things you spend your time doing during a normal day. When could you take the opportunity to tell someone about Jesus during your day?

PRAY

Ask God to make you aware of opportunities He gives you to tell or show others the love of Jesus. Ask Him to help your actions and the way you live to match the words you say.

I AM NOT ASHAMED

For I am not ashamed of the gospel, because it is the power of God for salvation to everyone who believes, first to the Jew, and also to the Greek.—Romans 1:16

Dexie wanted to bring her Bible to school, but she was afraid it was against the rules and she would get in trouble. She also wanted to invite her friends to join her at church on Wednesday nights, but what if her friends thought church was boring and laughed at her for going? Dexie was excited to learn more about Jesus. She wanted to share that excitement with her friends and tell them about how Jesus forgave her sins and promised her eternal life. But she was also a little embarrassed to let people know.

God does not want us to be ashamed or embarrassed to tell others about Him. In Romans 10:14, the Bible asks how people can know about God unless they are told. Of course, the answer is they won't know. Although sometimes God reveals Himself directly to people, most of the time He uses us—His people—to do it. It is our job to proclaim the good news!